BREATH ENOUGH

Vivian Teter

BREATH ENOUGH

Vivian Teter

WOLF RIDGE PRESS

ISBN   978-0-9818029-2-3
        0-9818029-2-3

Library of Congress Control Number: 2015956593

Book design, cover art, and frontispiece by Jeremy Thornton
Painted gourd in frontispiece and used in cover art by Carolyn K. Teter
Photo of gourd by Sharon Swift

Special thanks to Susan Marie Powers, first reader,
and Joan Baranow, gifted editor

WOLF RIDGE PRESS

350 Parnassus Avenue, Suite 900
San Francisco, CA 94117

www.wolfridgepress.com

for Carolyn Keth Teter

with love and gratitude to Joseph Polansky,
Margaret Devaney, the Brethren in Lititz,
Linda Reis, Julia Ruane-Smith, Paul Teter,
and my parents, Jacob and Shirley

ACKNOWLEDGMENTS

The author would like to thank these journals and anthologies in which the following poems appeared:

Anglican Theological Review: "Toward Ripening"

Artemis Journal: "The Tenth Dress," "Postcard," and "Together with You, Stranger" (originally a single poem titled "Postcard")

Asheville Poetry Review: "Rope, Sign, Edge"

The Best of Toadlily Press: New and Selected Poems: "Ode Against Falling"

The Cortland Review: "Caesura"

Edge by Edge: "Translating A Bridge" and "First Letter, Folded Close" (originally "Across the Street All Autumn")

Jefferson Monthly: "Tessera: Mimosa, Oak" (originally "Redwoods")

Passages North: "Treasured Story: The Prom Dress" (originally "Late")

Poetry East: "When to Sing," "UnSonnetting," and "Breath Enough"

The Poet's Almanac: "Breath Enough"
(*The Poet's Almanac* is associated with *Poetry East*)

Other Voices International Poetry Project: "On the Virtual Sill, On the Blue Hum"

Spoon River Poetry Review: "First Letter, Folded Close"
(originally "Across the Street All Autumn")

Contents

III

I

The glory of the Infinite reveals itself by
what it is capable of doing in the witness.

– Emmanuel Levinas, *Ethics and Infinity*

/

And keen through wordy snares to track
Suggestion to her inmost cell....
So word by word, and line by line....

– Alfred, Lord Tennyson, *In Memoriam A.H.H.*

Of Narrative and Neuron

To be flesh is to be *(by turn sweet*
 and terrifying) narrative:

    clasping hands as we walked unfurled
                that line of shore. Then curved

    back to tense, huddling
                in wind roaring.

/

What our kind wanted: to run fast, run light, run far
    from every declension, any last scene.

Then late *(very late)*: by fire, by grasp
    of stone honed, by reed, by stylus of bone:

    neurons flared and forged
    a cortical pathway. Synapses sparked.

/

    Letter-makers, word-bearers, we could soar
free of sequence and cessation:

    is this the way our song *(write yes)*
    forever rises?

Translating a Bridge

Damn in-the-dark   scratch
    & handscrawl.

   Is it
      salve or *salvage?*

  Seek, singe, or
   singing?

     Hurry to translate
  before brink
of day.

The Quarrel

Like a question mark
flipped on its side,
that line of stitches arcs.
Like two lips lashed tight,
that one mute seam careens:

clears your right ear's tip
then whips upward, swerves
to forehead's edge.
What map or gasp, what
border torn, ablaze—

—first drawn in dark ink
then signed with initials:
a surgeon's guide for cutting
from the correct lobe
that tumor deep in a maze.

Head high, shorn and hatless,
you stroll store aisles,
choose candles for dad's
eightieth cake. Some turn. Some
stare. In full glory, you swear

sister, a quarrel with this,
your loud half-crown
of fiery thorns.

Onerous Citizenship

Of the women:
not her
and not her

but her. Perhaps
behind the rib
in the lung

perhaps
over the lung
in the breast.

Look again:
not her, and no
not her, but her.

And the men too:
not him, but him—

here, deep in the gut
and again

not him, but next to him
—there, on the tongue

in the throat. Stripped
of citizenship
in the kingdom

of the well, these men
enter
—these women enter

that country of onerous
citizenship. Can we see

behind the curtains drawn
room to room
in the centers of infusion

their faces taken
wrists strapped
each with a number

can we speak
what we cannot hear
above the screen's hum

the monitors' beep
steady as registers
clicking open and shut

ward after ward this
stripping and stripping

of the utterly stripped.

Tessera: Mimosa, Oak

So far from our childhood
trees —

mimosa I sat in hours
cradling the neighbors' white cat

oak you swung from
over the creek, your body for moments

holding nothing, high above water, held
by the honey-close August air.

Caesura

We knew the odds,
thin and flimsy as a single
honeybee wing, that chance
at shrinkage. And even then
any bargain wouldn't keep:
there would be sudden flight
into glass.

But dazzling between
petals lit by spring
we laughed as we fit our lips
to the small heaven
of a shared cone of ice cream,
that afternoon all the films shone
a calm and cloudless sky.

First Letter, Folded Close

When the days bring
no schedule
other than medications

When few visit
and you sit in a lawn chair
under the tulip poplar

gazing darkly then shyly
at the edges of a blue sky
quizzical in its brilliance:

the sun itself praises you
the wind (old nuzzler) comes close

morning unfolds a quilt frayed but bright
with late summer threads

and the leaves begin to hum
in their going

drowning the growl of a distant machine
and dropping low golden vowels all around you

intimate
as that first letter opened long ago

and folded close at heart,
carried this far.

Treasured Story: The Prom Dress

From college you called Dad,
just in the door from work.
You needed a dress you forgot
for your big spring dance
only three days away.

Dad washes his hands,
finds and folds the gown
into its box, and then,
in coal-darkened overalls,
arrives at the UPS office

ten to six. The UPS lady
frowns, she scowls,
this cardboard isn't
sturdy enough. So he leaves
your dress on the counter

and when you tell this story
his next move becomes
a treasure for decades:
in the dumpster outside,
snatching at boxes in his wild

love, the steel lid slams,
dropping him in darkness to his knees.
But he is your hero, he wakes
minutes later to a warmth in his head,
he ties his handkerchief over the bleeding

that will require seven stitches, climbs out
with a new box, and calm at the counter
repacks your dress.
Though it is closing time, the lady,
wide-eyed, silent now

waits for him to finish. She waits
for you, who will dance
dress swirling, three nights from now
dancing and dancing
past any reasonable hour.

Rebound (Amygdalan)

Blood is toxic to neurons.
– Jill Bolte Taylor

Like a circuit worn and wound deep
in ancient amygdala

       reptilian
       silent

it elides
toward its appointed time.

       On cue
       the tea cup

drops
from your shattered hand.

The Neurosurgeon

for Dr. William Monacci

Weekends he walks the woods
watching for buntings and vireos,

hand and eye steady
to follow wings flitting

tree to tree. He trains
his vision on the barely

perceptible tracery
of a wren nesting.

When a branch lashes
and hawk talons

fill both lenses
he does not flinch.

Through everything
he stands listening

hard and long
for distant song.

Parsing

Glio: urgency to amass
sans glee

blastoma: mouth that cannot
be filled, ever

Multi: uncoiling vein after vein,
pipelining a personal supply

forme: to ensure its core
disconnection.

Glioblastoma
Multiforme:

A nine-syllable sentence
against harmony, an expertly

shifting, relentless, one-way
gain. An unmooring of words

from history and meaning.
In the end, all balance lost.

Elephants Fighting

Dut says, *In my country we keep our old or sick ones with us.* He
watches me sort stacks of claims on my desk at school. *I can build
a Dinka branch and palm house for you and your sister.* Her room
in rehab totals $55,000 a week. *In my village, when my grandfather
wandered down to the river, the women washing the clothes called out
to him Dut Akech, Dut Akech do you need washing also?* Insurance
rejects rehab's claim with this note: all miscellaneous charges must
be itemized. *The women sing sometimes when they wash. That day my
grandfather followed their song back.* Patient's responsibility: $55,000.
This year's claims: $1.2 million.

Dut shakes his head, clicks his tongue: *The elephants have not finished
fighting. My grandmother always sang a song, I remember how this song
ended: When there is nothing left, the people laugh at the ones who twist
and twist*

*trying to twist anything
from nothing.*

Slow Dancing

Our steps clumsy now, strapped
each to each, you dipping
then lifting your left leg
from its dragging,
me lagging half a beat.

Nonetheless we dance
and strangely sway
toward safety of a table.
You pass the bread
with your one good hand.

My two swoop to catch spoon,
to flutter napkin to your lips,
and like this we move together
through days off-kilter,
fast disappearing.

And when your good hand quivers,
then quakes and strays,
we curse together the spilt soup,
cry out loud at the honey pot
toppled.

What you cannot fathom,
my eyes reveal. What I cannot face,
you will.

II

...cancer is still perceived against all evidence as a natural illness.... As long as cancer remains an individual rather than a communal disease, as long it is buffered by cultural fear of suffering and death, stigma can be the only response.... Slippery military metaphors insist that individuals, rather than the culture, suffer from cancer and that cancer can be fought—battled—and represented as outside of the very culture that produces it.

– S. Lochlann Jain, *Malignant: How Cancer Becomes Us*

Tessera: Missive

Late strange language
of wind // spitting
honeybee

wing
after // wing

Erasure

When I returned in the morning,
I found you //no //longer who you had been.

You sat in pajamas// top soaked with sweat shame cerebral fluid//
with dried anger mucus tears// with spit terror hours of loss

of sobbing// with no tissue no washcloth nothing within reach
of your one good arm. Left in your locked wheelchair // far

from call bell/light switch/water glass//
medicine/phone/fire alarm//

doorknob.
In seven hours// stripped //crushed

utterly// of all you had become. There is no word now
//no touch //that will unbreak the globe of your broken

dignity. // No soft sweater/no bright scarf will bring
back what has been stripped. Your eyes//

of all spark and gleam//
looted now.

Rope, Sign, Edge

In the next room, and in the next facility, and the next, I line sills
with the gourds you hand-painted, I tape copies of your college
degrees to the wall, I put this picture of you at the head of your bed:
smiling brave and alone in a sunny field, white bouquet of tulips and
daisies in hand, wedding gown billowing.

//

The rope is strong, braided, silky. It is white. I tie it carefully around
your left wrist, fasten your cell phone. I punch a hole in cardboard,
scrawl, loop rope, sling this sign over one rail of your bed: "Under no
circumstance is this phone to be moved from Carolyn's reach."

I cover the room's white with photos of your son. I tell everyone you
worked nights in Micro not even six months ago, I work against their
monitors and charts, their fast hands and eyes whittling you to birth
date, to blood count. I hold out your gourds like exotic creatures, like
talismans, toward all who enter your room.

//

I think at last I have learned my lesson. But nothing stops the
white fire of these tile hallways, the machinery's whisper and click
Quicker, quick! Nurses, aides teeter on a volcanic lip, a hiss, *more
beds, less time.* Pushed by administrators pushed by stockholders by
bottom lines by sleek paths up to yachts and jets for the far-away few,
these nurses and aides are dangerous. And in danger. Something
rumbles. rumbles with each step they take. Compassion costs. most
have nothing. nothing shored up. Something heavy. rumbles tired.
beneath each. then rocks under all our steps and groans through
every wall buckling all the walls now, floor onto floor collapsing, bed
careening toward the window. I scream *sister,* I scream *more rope.*

What kind //   //
have we become//   //pushed to the edge

What kind of country //   //have we
become //   // pushed farther //   //and farther

 // one //
from   //   // another.

Harvests

How I feasted on the beets
you'd send for Christmas, glistening
deep garnet in their Mason jars
against crescent moons of onion.
I'd eat half a quart at once.

And the tomatoes,
rich with pulp and seed,
steaming against the frosty evening
—salty and sweet, teasing the tongue.
Take pity come winter, I would implore,

and send me the treasures
of your garden and kitchen,
bright sunlight of peaches
to thaw the dead of December.
So season after season, sister,

you mastered the metrics
of wind and sun and rain,
hoeing your lines in the soil,
growing a mortal poetry
of sweat and love and hands full of light.

Tessera: Braille

all along your belly your thighs your skin blistering blindly
my fingertips tamp the flow. gauze. touch. ever so lightly the skin
wet but not broken skin wet but not broken not broken not weeping
from the drugs but from above honey from above honey-salve
dropping from above honey holding you. holding you.
holding you close.

Curse

The young nurse scolds you
as she lifts your left, paralyzed
hand and arm to wash them.

"Sleeping Sally
sounds much nicer.
That's what you need to say."

Two days after the last
brain surgery, you named
that arm "Dead Fred"

and "Dead Fred"
remained your curse
to the end.

On the Same Side:
Words Wrung & Wrought

You honed tongue and glare
to sharpest arrow, our softest tissue
—that curled mass knit with neurons—
your target: "Stop that—

stop touching my hand.
It's you—
not the nurse. If you'd
just leave

I could swallow this pill—
just get out
now." We learned fast
how Decadron wrecks and roars

its price to keep a cancerous tumor
coiled back from bone of your skull.
And no, we could not stop
day after day lying to you:

"Your eyelashes look so thick
so pretty again, they do.
Yes your face does still
look like you—it does too."

Scalped, scalpeled, we lobbed words
bladed, bloodied, skinned
words gleaming or dug-up rusted
words glass-thin or brass-knuckled

words wrought and flung raw
against steel breastplate, against greaves,
flint-sparks to light us through
such warped pitch and heave.

From Field to Field

A year after your husband
betrayed and broke you,
you harvested
fifty birdhouse gourds.
Sky-blue squares floating
on waves of mauve, you lifted
your first finished one high,
showing me the holes
you carved for air, explaining
the careful drying and cleaning,
how the skin, hardened, absorbs
pigments, the ease of paint flowing
all winter like one long afternoon,
your quick wrist and brush turning
every curve steady and sure
until countless snowdrops
floated in a copper sea, dusky purple
bloomed sun-rays, and lightning crossed
loops of tangerine,
zigzags of green—

everything was reeling
yet each pattern and shade emerged
clear and bright in turn, each held
by a firm black meandering
of a border you could follow
only as you came up and crossed
one field over to another.

Arriving at *If*

Blink one eye *if*.
Bend your right thumb *if*.
And *if*_____, *if*,
shift, quiver, lift _____
stagger, wobble, stunned
we bolt into this strained
land of *If*.

This is not the *if*
we knew
years and years back
shouting in our shared bedroom
deep into night's open window
"What if
      we go to the moon what if

we wake up in our dreams
what if our breasts never grow and if
we skip school in this land of the free
and so what if we eat too much cake"
—that if always companioned back then
by *what*
      or *so*:

        So what if
there's no knight on horseback,
sword high, galloping toward us
_____ and no trail
of crumbs left now to lead us
back through amber fields
to even a dream of home——————

The Oncologist

for Dr. Samuel Kerr

On trial for the vanishing,
today you have nothing left

except this: you turn
your back to the screen

flashing its white numbers,
its codes for procedure or disease,

and you enter a zone unknown,
moving slowly, within inches

to sit, face to face,
with this woman who waits.

Today you let her eyes find
their answers in yours,

yours perfectly mirroring
hers: yours, hers, the deepest

they have ever been
in a light shivering

and breathless: both open,
both seeking

that elusive neural signature
of the yet-to-be-

fathomed and freed
will that marks

her, that marks you,
so wholly human.

Of Seeds Salvaged

Like sharp   sunlit   barely visible   silver-gold seeds
blown over thousands of miles   of pale desert sand
then washed   rippling across skins   of ocean waves
your words   Bul   float down   these white tile corridors

and slip into mind's   maze: *"I could not understand*
when he was older   and stronger   running just ahead
why those soldiers would shoot my brother   and not shoot
me   and for what reason   could they not take my brother

like they took only some life of me?"   Bul   you gave
one grain   of your huge grief that day   and today
it finds me   and I carry it   close and alive
into my dying sister's room   still learning

how long   like a lost syllable   the seed waits
holding the tongue of the bloom   toward safe opening.

Postcard

slipped into a book in a waiting room.
At first I struggle with smeared whorls
and faint waves of smudged ink, then sink
to wonder at the lack of date and legible place
of origination. But in bold and easy blue
these letters stroke toward me: *"I painted snow
when I wasn't shoveling."* The blizzard slowing,
a span of field blanketed, and snow-capped bales
brushed warm in gold and lavender note a sun
that's just begun its long, unbroken journey.

After Ryan Russell's "Snow-Capped Bales"

Of Jewels

*In Kakuma I finally could not sleep. Each morning I learned
the boy on either side of me had died.* – John Lueth

With sudden passion
John Lueth, the quietest,
turns to me:

"There is always a jewel.
Everywhere there are jewels.
You have to find your jewel."

That is what I heard.
This is what he said: "Dear ones,
you have to find your Julie."

At Kakuma he sat in the dust
day after day, writing *eighteen*
in the form's blank for age

though he was only sixteen.
Day after day in sun he sat
before the U.N. tent

so small a boy,
who would believe
he could be eighteen?

He sat before her at dawn.
He sat before her at nightfall.
He sat trapped between two words:

burial, or *eighteen.*
Finally in the thirty-first week
she too learned and miraculously

wrote *eighteen.* And this is what he said:
"Her name was Julie.
Everywhere I have since been

there is always a Julie."
Yes, John Lueth, yes. Always
such Julies, such jewels.

Vanquishing *If*

Against this multiplication of *If* by *If*
this tsunami of *If,* this torch of *If*

against this bullet-spray of *If*
this swirling debris of *If*

this amputating
shrapnel of *If*——

against this derecho of *If*
this drought of *If,* this ice-fall

this virus leaping———
against this pandemic, metastatic *If*

we gather together
and we hold.

III

Because every brain is unique in its neurological wiring, every brain is unique in its ability to recover from trauma.

– Jill Bolte Taylor, *My Stroke of Insight*

/

Their great longing sprouted wings,
Needing to search the sky.

– Shams-ud-din Muhammad Hafiz
(trans. Daniel Ladinsky)

Simon's Essay

You stop after your sentence "My shoes gone, the soles of my feet burned away, I could not walk one other step." Then in frustration you tell me how really you had no hope. I nod. We are caught together in a small trap today. A wealthy donor is offering pharmacy school tuition, but first you must write about your experience of hope. He requests a theme of hope that prevails over all tribulation. He will read your essay at an awards banquet.

You shake your head. You lost even the fire to live, you say. Not even the begging and wailing of your little sister and brother could make you move. How then did you survive, I ask.

Down the line of boys the crying reached the ears of one strong and older boy who came and quieted the children, hoisted you onto his back, and carried you the next twenty miles. Someone at the next stop had medicine, someone kept singing, there was a tree with shade, somehow a U.N. Jeep arrived.

You take up your pen. "Hope many times is a well that dries. I write to you, sir, my hope did not prevail. It was not the hope of others, only a thing I can never describe. Some could continue to walk to escape bullets and hunger. I sat down to die. I can attest I saw in the face of my sister and brother great fear. And I can promise for you the mercy shown to me by one who could not walk past a dying boy without trying to lift him from the teeth of the hyena.

Thank you. Simon Deng."

For Lee, Who Shines

down corridor after corridor
through room after room.

You looked in on us
our first freezing night

of paralysis, and you did not
turn away or ignore the tears.

You took our hands in yours,
the flame of your spirit

thawing, nourishing.
When we could see nothing

you gazed at us beyond our torn
faces, our lost tongues.

You returned to us the gift
of our names.

When to Sing

Damage the left hemisphere:
you cannot speak.

Damage the right:
you cannot sing.

I wheeled you to the chapel
you could still

speak then
you said:

I heard you sing. I saw you weep
as you stood singing.

It's good for you, that
deep. Don't forget.

Your right hemisphere all scar
cancer & riddle

I had to sing when
defenseless

your songs stole
far, so far

so softly
gone.

Tessera: Last Testament

No cause, no cure
in trembling orange
crayon on one door
in a neurotrauma ward

your last written note
quick with your wit:
And from now on
I will be sleeping in.

Ode Against Falling

That letter like a heavy
stone in the throat,
but odd: the center
hollow,
        bitter "o"
                falling "o."

This letter a hard stick
            gnarled at the far
end,
    the dead end,
            its knuckle
                of debris.

The next a vowel that like steel
        sleeps across a chest its heavy beam.
It was supposed to be rest,
                steady breaths
                        not
such uneasy wheezing.

Lone letters
    scattered,   lost
from their ode,
            look how
the hand trembles now, fingers
    search and pick

to gather, to garner
to assemble, to make

some thing, something of such
disarray. Such falling away.

Breath Enough

Your voice soft now *please* as softest
tuft floating free

of torn flesh. *Please don't,*
don't turn me.

And when a hand lifts a straw
to your lips, you whisper

 Thank you
—breath enough

for the only dignity
not stripped:

your words

uncrushed
rising cloudward.

Bargaining

Years back when your hand
held strong and steady,
your quick fingers aligned violet
with lime, indigo with crimson
as you grieved a marriage gone.
You protested but I persisted,
gathering those gourds in a basket
where they beamed into stalls
in the barns of the PA Gourd Festival,
artist after artist asking, "Are these
for sale?" You didn't believe anyone
would want your beauty again.

When no one would take you
—too young, too wrecked,
last on a list too full with elders,
and too heavy to lift after too many
meds doubled your flesh— I armed
myself with those gourds.
Over applications placed down
on mahogany desks (your assets
under penalty of law all listed)
I lifted gourd after gourd: look!
her hands made this and more:
this shines in her, and this one:

gold and copper medallions
bright coins of color
bargaining for a chance,
a clean place, some
restoration of a life
drawing too soon
into a field
unbearably
white.

The Tenth Dress, Word-Woven

In Modoc legend, Kumush the great father
cannot bear his daughter's plea for her tenth dress.

"But Father, your words wove
  this dress first, humming every inch
  of its buckskin into a song of white shells.
  You taught me its meaning many summers ago.
  Why won't you now bring it to me?"

"What is wrong with this dress, the one
  for after your bath? Or this one,
  for digging roots? How small now the dress
  for you at seven! But take this one: the one
  for gathering wood." Like Kumush my father

  holds tight to the tenth dress. Each week
  he brings instead a new t-shirt,
  each week he searches store aisles
  for a larger pair of slippers
  though she will not walk again.

  But to be by his youngest daughter's side
  Kumush finally sees what he must do:
  "When I give you this tenth dress, my child,
  I shall travel with you. I shall leave my body
  on the earth, but I shall not die."

"Father, are your eyes closed?
Only those with closed eyes who lie down
and become dry bone, only they can see
to follow the path of the setting sun."
And so my father dozes

in my sister's room, facing the window
where the sky flares into fire and fades
Pennsylvania farm fields. Shared breaths
in a small room, see how each night
he leaves the nursing home

and each sunrise he returns
bringing her spirit back. Like Kumush
he makes himself small, so small
my sister slips him into a crack far up
in a corner of the great house below the world.

It is a world of drums and speech,
high voices and sweet music that rings
beyond human ears. And come daylight
she vanishes, come dawn she disappears,
singing a song falling soft on his skin as rain.

And so my father journeys back, waking
in a body he has carried eighty-three years.
His arms now empty of dresses,
he groans from some vast deep all loss
of language

then wild-eyed, his palms upward and burning
he rushes toward my arms the heavy blanket
that wrapped her last breath.
My hands taking it
translate from flame

what must be passed forward:
the secret of how to carry with us
all light from those who came before,
with greatest care, and in praise
for as long as we walk this earth.

After C.J. Brafford's "Kumush and His Daughter," a Modoc creation story in
Dancing Colors: Paths of Native American Women

UnSonnetting

What struggle to escape?
                        – John Keats

Blossom on blossom opening branch after bare branch
mouth of tulip, lips of crocus, cusp and cup unburying
blade after green blade all thrusting up
fist after petalled fist twisting, blinking to sky, unpetalling

and endless this multiplication, these layers, this fury of roots
and tumor threading and weaving one song, one note
wedding your cheek to pale petal, paler unblinking
                        but calling now, calling untongued

so we too fall, calling out your many new names
there and over there, a whisper, a lifting, trembling of vein and leaf
rising to the sun's hand then riding, riding the shade's long back
—everywhere and at once you draw near

                        your skin of finest petals gathered
                        shimmering upward, wind-borne, stunning.

On the Virtual Sill, On the Blue Hum

Dearest, when loomingly
midday sun darkens

and the bell of this red horizon
rings its cut-off tongue

like a thick, hot wire sparking
over steel and asphalt

—indeed, rings deep violet
 like a noose

with its noisy megabyte news
of the cutters

and
the cut—

then, carefully, on my belly
pulling this body over damp soil

with fingers stretched
prehistorically taut,

with both hands I reach
for you, Darling:

plucked and culled
tested and tasted

vowel by exquisite
vow. Your every consonant

clasped, dreamt, sipped
like an ancient wine of syllables

from a glass shattering,
your each dawning cry

cradled, coddled, escorted
through all the fluorescent hours

courted, carried, week into month
morning to evening. Curved and tucked.

On the virtual sill, on the blue hum
of screen, in blood and synapse:

assembled and reassembled.
Shouted whispered fretted.

Welded. Wielded. Burning solar
in the mortar of a pre-dawn skull

until,
finally,

this construction:
one uncorrodible sentence

launched against all gilded
and fraudulent sentences,

against any genocide
and every extinction.

Rare and dearest: two worlds
caving, the next careening:

whirl and wing, unimprisonable.
Brace and hold.

The Question

Dawn light woke me with the question:
Your blue knit cap, where is it?
—the one you wore after your first
craniotomy, after your second, after
"damn this third cranie"

and now I can't find it
the blue cap that travelled continents
of interior weather and survived
in the last four months alone twenty-five
ambulance rides, five

hospital room changes in the two days
before Christmas, your blue cap jaunty
with the leaping rabbit in white ceramic
pinned high on the suture side, journeying along
for every trip to rehab, to ER, back to rehab

to New Year's in neuro-trauma
then rehab, then back to ER, back
and back until we lost count finally, lost
that cap somewhere before the road going uphill
to the nursing home, sometime after your paralysis.

"Remember when we moved from Oklahoma
to Maryland," you asked, your mind unlinking,
spinning random eddies. "Yes, I remember,
I was ten and you were six." "Five, I was five I
can still see that rabbit it's fast."

You closed your eyes. By your bed while you slept
I wondered what you saw from the right back seat,
if you saw what I saw from the left—
I didn't know you remembered that rabbit.
Did you watch the road waver with heat

the cars ahead zigzag, in the clearing
  a rabbit running
  toward the yellow line, my breath slowing
  its front paws above that yellow line
breath zeroing tighter

  then rushing loose with its burst
  of movement forward.
  Our car passed, I looked back,
  another car slicing my view
but I spotted that rabbit seconds enough

  didn't I, to see it running
  oh to see it running with yellow
  yellow all yellow where its hind legs
  should have been.
  You were six

  and at ten I pressed my hands
  against the hot glass, wordless.
Dawn light woke me with the question
of your blue knit cap and the question
you never asked, sparing me.

Little blue cap, little threadbare survivor,
whoever now finds you will find
high on the suture side that rabbit darting
across the sky, snow-bright, leaping brilliant
through soft blue night.

Joyful Lessons

The brain has this amazing ability to find happiness even when the memories of it are gone.
　　　　　　　　　　　　　　　– Charles Duhigg, *The Power of Habit*

I. TEACHING DUT TO USE REVERSE

It would be a '92 Grand Marquis
the church donates.
Dut, quick and sure
in the middle of the Nile,
but this boat?
His joyful fearlessness
makes a caged hummingbird
of my heart.

We move backward in half-moons
the length of the empty lot,
chassis bobbing.
It grows dark much too soon, I think.
Or maybe not— Dut aims headlights
confidently forward, his smile
flashing like fireworks
as he blazes from sight.

II. Simon's Firsts

When his first car breaks down
near Broad Creek on 264,
Simon simply leaves it—no problem—
and walks three hours back
to his apartment in Ghent.

*

Simon drives downtown to pay
in person his first parking ticket.
How unbelievable when he comes out
and a police officer stands writing another.
"Sir, I just paid that ticket!"
He laughs now when he tells us the story.

Together with You, Stranger

Yes, together with you, stranger
and spirit so kin, I too by turn
will now spend my days
painting the snow
when not shoveling it,
painting cloud after cloud
when back aches
from digging hard earth,
and if silence looms too long,
shaping sounds both bright and dark
into song so loud
snow will shatter back to flakes
and fly. Oh we will make
at last the ground flash silver
as it meets the shovel's
swift cold blade.

Tessera: Blazed Throat

hung
in our December
window // hummingbird //

wings thrumming

Psalm

The human brain has 100 billion neurons, each with ten thousand connections to other neurons. – National Geographic

Most beautiful of bodily cells
connecting the invisible electrical
to our heavy flesh: *let us praise*

Sending forth dendrite after dendrite
from your core, branchtip brinking
branchtip to hallow a space, a synapse: *let us praise*

Harnessing all impulse into leap,
into seek, into synchronous
synthesis and syntax with which   *we now praise*

Yours the tie that weds intent to hand
Yours the cord that binds grace to syllable   *praise to lip*
to current to circuits surging and lifting

praising ceaselessly your machinery and   *mystery most sweet*
your architecture of intersection
of resurrection

*praise to your miracle
of linkage and connection.*

Toward Ripening

A taste of God
resides in the flesh
of a fully ripe peach

so that,
sweating out there among the trees,
bending and twisting your body
row after row toward the fruit, you remind us
there was once a sweet deal struck on Earth—

to taste the full richness,
to have a chance at ripening:
each of us hungering to reach a peak
of sweetness, and each generation's sweetness
cresting, building, wanting a lasting light, down here
among us, on this Earth—

and until then, you motion to us:
come, taste the deep
mystery of this summer's peach
so that, at the time of having to leave it all—
all that divinely fleshed beauty, all
that was carried forward and won, all
that waits at hand, undone—

leaving it will not be
so hard, not so bitter, holding
to a memory of sweetness as we fall,
our mouths filling with sugar
our mouths, even now, filling
with song.

About the Author

Vivian Teter holds an M.F.A. in poetry from the University of Arizona and a B.A. in English from Hollins University. Her chapbook *Translating a Bridge* was published in 2007 by Toadlily Press of Chappaqua, New York in its Quartet Series *Edge by Edge*. She has received two Pushcart Prize nominations and several fellowships from the Virginia Center for the Creative Arts. One of her poems was selected by the Poetry Society of Virginia and the MetroRail Public Arts Project to be incorporated into a permanent art installation at a new D.C. metro station to open in 2016. She teaches at Virginia Wesleyan College in Norfolk, Virginia.